This book belongs to:

# Happy Valentine's Day Monkey & Friends

Coloring Book

Mary Lou Brown & Sandy Mahony

Love is in the air
BE MY VALENTINE

WiTh
Love

BE MY VALENTINE
MILK

BE MY VALENTINE
Love

LOVE

VALENTINE'S
DAY

adventurelearningpress.com

www.ingramcontent.com/pod-product-compliance
Lightning Source LLC
Chambersburg PA
CBHW081807280526
45789CB00008B/3036
* 9 7 8 1 5 4 1 3 9 9 7 1 6 *